One World

Going to School

Amanda Rayner

W

FRANKLIN WATTS

LONDON • SYDNEY

Note
about the series
One World is designed to encourage young readers to find out more about people and places in the wider world. The photographs have been carefully selected to stimulate discussion and comparison.

First published in 2007 by Franklin Watts
338 Euston Rd, London NW1 3BH

Franklin Watts Australia
Hachette Children's Books
Level 17/207 Kent St, Sydney, NSW 2000

© Franklin Watts 2007

Editor: Caryn Jenner
Designer: Louise Best
Art director: Jonathan Hair
Map: Ian Thompson
Reading consultant: Hilary Minns, Institute of Education, Warwick University

Acknowledgements: Robert Aberman/Hutchison: 19. Toby Adamson/Still Pictures: 13. Derek Cattani/Eye Ubiquitous: 18. David Cumming/Eye Ubiquitous: 27. Mark Edwards/Still Pictures: 14, 17, 20, 25. Chris Fairclough/Eye Ubiquitous: 11. Ron Giling/Still Pictures: cover, 24. Felix Greene/Hutchison: 16. Paul Harrison/Still Pictures: 8. Thomas Kelly/Still Pictures: 21. Skjold/Eye Ubiquitous: 9. Mike Southern/Eye Ubiquitous: 10. Liba Taylor/Hutchison: 22. Penny Tweedie/Still Pictures: 15, 23. Patrick Ward/Corbis: 26. Julia Waterlow/Eye Ubiquitous: endpapers, 12.

A CIP catalogue record for this book is available from the British Library

ISBN: 9780749676575

Dewey Classification: 371

Printed in Malaysia

Franklin Watts is a division of Hachette Children's Books.

Contents

At school

All over the world, children go to school. At school, you **study** and learn lots of different things. You can make friends, too.

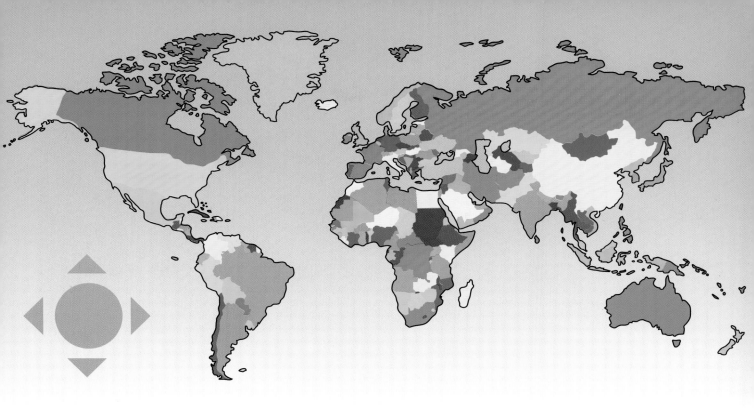

This is a **map** of all the **countries** in the world. Read this book to find out about schools in different places around the world.

▶ This girl is studying at school. In this book, you will see children doing lots of different things at many different schools.

Getting to school

Many children walk to school.
These girls in Kenya walk through
fields in the countryside to get
to their school.

These children in the United States walk to school with a grown-up. The school patrol uses her flag to help the children cross the road safely.

Different schools

This small school in Peru is on an island in the middle of a big lake. Children travel to school on boats from villages around the lake.

This school in Britain was built about a hundred years ago. The teachers and lessons have changed since then, but the buildings are the same.

Classrooms

At school, children usually have lessons in a classroom. In this classroom in Brazil, boys and girls sit at desks in neat rows.

In hot weather, some children have classes outside. These children in Sudan are having their lesson sitting under a tree.

Teachers

Teachers help children to learn.
This teacher in Haiti helps a girl
to write in her exercise book.
The other children in the class
work quietly on their own.

At storytime, a teacher reads
to the class and asks questions
about the story. During this
storytime in Australia, children
are raising their hands to
answer a question.

Reading and writing

Children around the world learn to read and write in their own **languages**. This girl in China is writing Chinese characters. Each character stands for a whole word or idea.

These children in Burkina Faso read and write in French. On their chalkboards, they have written "la terre", which means "the earth".

Finding information

Some schools have **libraries** where children can find **information** on lots of different subjects. These children in Ireland are working together to collect information about a topic.

Children use **computers** in schools to find information on the **Internet**. This school is in Israel.

In the playground

At school, it is important to exercise the body as well as the brain! These children in Indonesia are doing exercises in the school playground.

At break time, children can have fun in the playground. These children in India are playing games on a climbing frame.

Lunch break

At lunchtime, many children eat together at school. These children in Thailand are having a hot school lunch made with rice and vegetables.

Some children take a packed lunch to school, in a bag or a lunchbox. These children in New Zealand sit outside to eat sandwiches and other food they have brought from home.

Special days at school

School concerts are very exciting. These children in Ghana are singing and playing the drum in their school concert. They have been practising for a long time.

School trips help children to
find out more about the world.
These children in Spain are on
a school visit to learn how to
look after the countryside.

Learning at home

In Australia, some children do not have a school nearby. They learn at home instead. They use computers and two-way radios to talk to their teachers.

◄ This boy in Russia is doing his homework. All over the world, children have homework to do after school. It helps them to practise what they have learned at school.

All around the world

All around the world, children go to school.

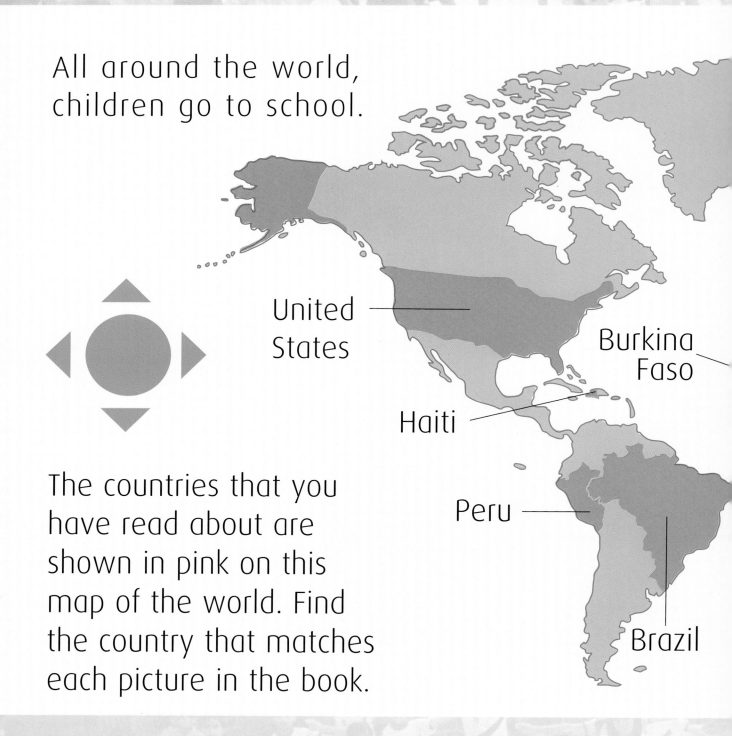

The countries that you have read about are shown in pink on this map of the world. Find the country that matches each picture in the book.

United States

Burkina Faso

Haiti

Peru

Brazil

Ireland

Russia

Britain Spain

Ghana

Israel

Sudan

India

China

Thailand

Indonesia

Kenya

Australia

New Zealand

29

Glossary

computer   a machine that stores information

countries   places with their own governments

information   facts

Internet   a way of looking for information on a computer

language   the words that people use to read, write and speak

library   a place where books are kept

map   a drawing that shows where places are

study   to spend time learning about a subject

Index